How to Get What You Want

In Your Life

Entrepreneur Book Series

M. Usman

Mendon Cottage Books

JD-Biz Publishing

Download Free Books!

http://MendonCottageBooks.com

Our books are available at

1. Amazon.com
2. Barnes and Noble
3. Itunes
4. Kobo
5. Smashwords
6. Google Play Books

Table of Contents

Preface

I want to congratulate you for your interest in this particular book titled, *How to Get What You Want in Life.*

This book will act as your greatest guide to attaining whatever it is that you want in your life, as it contains, in detail, the plans that will assist you to attain your goals.

When you mindfully focus to achieve certain goals, then this focus becomes an integral part of you. You can almost visualize what you will be feeling once you get that thing or whatever it is that you want. This feeling will never leave your thoughts until you are able to achieve the goal, be it education, money, a built body, or power. The list is truly endless. There are so many things that a person might want in his life, some are really important, while others are just straight down trivial and not worth the hustle.

Normally, most of the goals are usually hard to achieve, but do not be fooled into believing that they are unattainable. The difference that separates those who actually realize their goals and individuals who don't is not really immense. It's just the way they go about their goals that is different.

Ever heard of a song or a movie where the character states that you cannot get what you always want? Or how many times have you repeatedly heard such a statement being made? Well, you are about to understand the truth that such people forget to tell you.

This book will offer a broad spectacle about success and how any individual can use success to get whatever he desires in life. Its scope is diverse, and it relates to individuals seeking change. With this book, your possibilities will become endless.

People always dream of getting so many things in their life, especially the "impossible" things. However, especially during these times, if you want to achieve your goals, you will have to make certain changes in order to be successful.

This book will provide an intimate overview of a successful individual's daily itinerary and the habits that you need to emulate, in order to be prosperous in getting what you want in this world.

I. Success and Habits of a Successful Individual

Chapter # 1: Principles of Success

There are so many ways that individuals define success. In this detailed guide we will focus on how a person can become prosperous in getting what they want.

Being successful will generally increase your chances achieving your goals. As the wise folks usually state, opportunity favors the prepared mind. When you learn to observe the principles of success, you will have the skill and ability to improve the probabilities of achieving your own objectives.

Let's discuss the most relevant principals of fortunate people who often get what they desire:

Virtues

While you may want to achieve certain goals or objectives, you will have to develop certain virtues in order to realize your goals. These provide a compass direction towards the objectives that you want to realize. For example, if your goal is to visit Africa, then it will be vital for you to develop relevant exploration and travelling virtues that will ensure you have a comfortable and secure experience there. When you want something, the virtues you develop will compliment your skills and ultimately impart more meaning to the goals you want to achieve. Goals formulated on virtues, ensure that you remain rejuvenated for the pursuit. Take kindness for example; you always have all the time in your life to be kind. It costs you nothing to be kind and the returns on the investments you make based on kindness are unparalleled. This is mostly because when you treat others with kindness they will be more responsive to your demands.

Focus

Another key principle you need to understand if you want to be prosperous is focus. Most of the time, you fail to achieve your goals in life because you do not put enough focus in your endeavours. You should always view unattainable challenges as just cunningly concealed opportunities for development. If you decide to focus your resources and take up the challenges you face, you will be able to solve them yourself. This will relay improvement in your life and you will always maintain the path towards the right direction.

Do what you love

It's not always about the money. There is just so much out there that is more valuable than money. You need to understand that you have a superior purpose in life than just making money; this is the only way you can truly prosper. Seek fervour and let it always drive you to attain your goals.

Obstacles alienation

Avoid spending most of your time focussing on the exterior barriers that surround you. Do not, at any moment, let these obstacles become excuses in your life. However, the more visible and conscious you become of your internal obstacles, the easier it will be for you to dissolve them. You will begin to notice real change when the external barriers start to fade away.

Inspiration

You should understand that it's your responsibility to play a decisive role in making things happen the way you want them to in your life. You also need to understand that action separates dreams from deeds. In order to be able to achieve your objectives, you will be required to create your own vision, be expressive about it, and own it, so that you can propel yourself towards your goals.

Failure

Finally, we will discuss challenging matters that concern failure, especially when you fail to achieve your ambitions. Though you might not actually believe it, many successful people have experienced failure at some point in their lives. What you don't know yet is that these people were able to realize the key to failure. It provides the tools that help you to make things work so that you can get it right the next time.

Chapter # 2: What it Costs to Have a Successful Life

Success plays an important role in anyone who wants to be the guy who gets whatever he wants. In this section, we will uncover the real cost of success, so that we can discover how to really achieve our goals all the time.

Some of you, by now, are probably thinking about the monetary value of success. However, success is not measured in terms of monetary value. In fact, with this guide you will be able to learn about success without having to pay for anything. Particularly, you will learn how to use your life habits to pay for the cost of success. With these habits, you are assured of being a successful individual who is able to realize his goals recurrently. These habits include:

1. Waking up early

So many prosperous individuals are known to be early risers. This particular habit has more to do with the achievement of goals than you might be aware of. You need to be able to comprehend how waking up early attributes to success so that you can begin to embrace the habit itself. Larks usually start their day before everyone else, so they have time to act in response to others and also do some morning exercises. They have time for personal itinerary and this in turn reflects opulence in their life; they'll be happier, more proactive, and full of positivity.

2. Manage your own funds

Like other successful people who have been able to maintain their fortunate lives through admirable fund management skills, you should be able to manage your own funds wisely. Instead of being a spendthrift, you should always be on the lookout for sound investment opportunities. You should emulate how prosperous people save their money and remember to also set aside some funds in case of an emergency.

3. Preparing tomorrow's itinerary the night before

If you want accomplish specific objectives, you should always plan your schedule in advance. Most successful individuals are foresightful. In order to develop this habit and emulate it like a real pro, you will have to plan your tasks according to the relevance of each errand or task. This way you'll have enough time to actually do something you consider important by spending more time to accomplish that particular task.

4. Networking

In order to be prosperous in achieving personal objectives, you will have to understand the importance of networking. There are so many facts that prove the efficiency of networking. Through networking, the rate of unemployment has improved among youth in so many areas around the world. When you embrace the initiative of networking with others, you will be assured of budding innovativeness into your life. You will maturate to become a genuine and empathetic person, as opposed to being a critic who complains all the time.

5. Goal settings and visualization

As much as you may not want to believe it, you are required to do this on a regular basis in order to realize the objectives that you set. You should write down your goals, visions, and plans during the evening, so that the following day, you will be perfectly organized to undertake the challenges that await you. This is an excellent way to go about your life objectives.

6. Knowing how and when to say "No"

You need to practice your refusal skills appropriately, like Warren Buffet, if you really want to be fortunate. When you have mastered refusal skills, you will also have an idea of how to manipulate these skills to your own advantage. You need to be able to ignore harmful activities that do not only waste your time, but also damage your health. Refusal skills will ensure that you are focused enough to deal with important tasks that you need to accomplish.

Chapter # 3: Constructive Assessment Plan for a Successful Individual

The sole purpose of this section is to ensure that you are able to formulate a plan that will guarantee you remain fortunate in your pursuit to achieve your lifelong objectives. Constructive assessment plays an integral part in every successful person's life. You will be able to evaluate, control, and coordinate your daily routine to ensure that you maintain your successful reputation. The ultimate purpose of the plan is to ensure that you achieve your goals and ensure that your successful state remains progressive.

STEP 1: State what you want

You will state or indicate the goal that you want to achieve.

STEP 2: Identify and collect resourceful information

Look for reliable information through networking or individual research to know the preeminent path to use, in order to achieve your goal.

STEP 3: Evaluate your current assessment plan

If you feel that your current plan is not effective enough, then you will have to modify or completely alter it. Keep in mind that patience is the key to success.

STEP 4: Identify additional methods and plans

If you discover alternative ways that you can use to easily achieve your goals, please include them in the plan at this stage.

STEP 5: Execution and evaluation of the plan

This is the last and final stage where you will have to evaluate the results of your plan. If you got what you wanted, then the plan was a success, if not then you will have to develop another one and start over again.

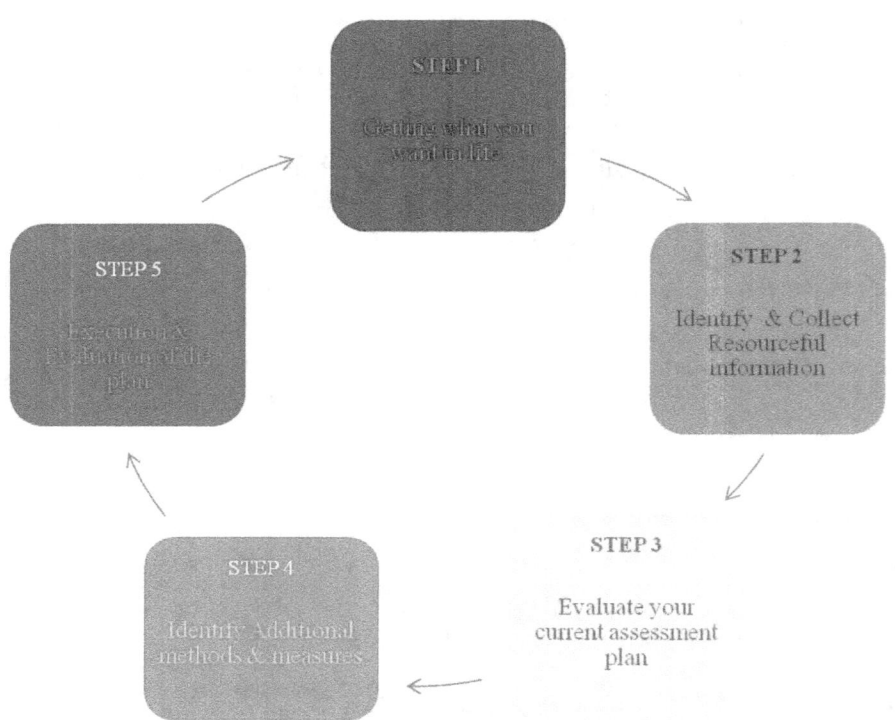

II. Concepts and Misconceptions about Success

Chapter # 4: Getting what you want; The Money Concept

A common misconception about success is that it involves having lots of cash in your bank account. While this may be partially true, success defines a lot more than just monetary value. Like Jim Blasingame, a contributor at Forbes states, "Success is not measured only by money and 'stuff.'"

In this chapter, we will discuss the difference between money and success, how they complement each other, and ultimately how you can use both money and success to achieve your ambitions.

Whenever you want to achieve a goal that requires the use of money, then you are going to have to do some kind of negotiation with another person. In this chapter, we will discuss more about how to be an excellent negotiator, so that you are able to get whatever it is that you want, by using shrewd negotiation skills.

These days, in order to be a notable negotiator, you will be required to embrace creative sales, marketing, and strategy skills. What usually happens is that you'll never get what you want in terms of price, but you are assured of getting what you negotiate for, so let's sharpen your negotiation skills.

Before we begin to discuss the relevant skills that you'll need to be a proper negotiator, you have to embrace certain concepts correctly, so that you are able to put the skills into proper practice .These concepts include:

Take action

Before you begin any business negotiations, the first thing that you will have to do is to know the total amount of money that you will need in order to even begin the negotiations. It is unwise to begin a negotiation when you do not have enough funds to purchase what you want. If you find yourself in this predicament, then you can decide to apply the following options:

- hold a fundraiser

- practice rejection therapy to build your confidence and remove the fear of asking for cash in case you do not have enough

Be informed

Before any transaction, it is a wise thing to always ask yourself whether you really have to spend money to achieve your goal. Most people often prefer to use money as an alternative means of achieving their goals, rather than using the proper means.

Understand

The common belief that you cannot achieve your intentions in life just because you don't have money is usually incorrect. This is just a red herring that masqueraders use to confuse others. You will have to ask yourself whether you are willing to pay the price for your goals. Everything has a price, but that price may not be actual cash. Also, you'll find that many people tend to talk about goals that they want to achieve only to forget about them later on. The fact that they do not follow up on them means that they were just merely talking and were not serious about what they said in the first place. People usually pursue their dreams differently. While others believe that they have to travel to different places in the world to achieve their goals, others usually prefer to put their focus on the intentions they have.

Make no mistake; both of these approaches do work, provided that you maintain consistency in your work.

Relevant Negotiation skill

1.   Identify your counterpart's agenda and embrace it.

In order to start the negotiation process, you will have to understand the other person's point of view. For example, you need to find out what your counterpart will view as a successful deal in order to know how you can make him feel better about the result of the transaction. In general, you need to empathize with the one you are doing business with in order to negotiate properly.

2.   Promote your story, not your standards.

The one that will have the best story between the two of you will always emerge as the winner. You should try your best to use your story to support the bids that you make. A good example of this concept is how American President Barrack Obama sold his story as a guy from humble backgrounds, while he negotiated with the citizens for the presidency seat during the presidential campaigns in 2008. Another former president, Sir Abraham Lincoln, also used this shrewd negotiation skill to win the presidential campaign. If you do not have a similar story that will help with the negotiation, you can come up with an equivalent to support your bid in terms of facts, figures, and the market reality.

3. Sandbagging.

It would be unfortunate for you to try sandbagging during the process of negotiation. Sandbagging simply means, when people downplay themselves in order to achieve an obscured objective from the matter. Many guys feel like they need to spend a lot of time bargaining with their counterparts in order to justify their bargaining skills. The bottom line is that you should steer clear of unnecessary spending by avoiding sandbagging in the first place.

4. Always be the first to make an offer.

Contrary to old beliefs of letting the other person state his price first, you should go first instead. When you do this you will be able to take control of the negotiation and set the parameters of the market reality.

5. Dealing with deadlock situations.

Suppose the negotiation process hits a deadlock, you will have to switch on your higher I.Q. process in order to disarm the other person. You can decide to ease off or even back off from the negotiation process for a couple of hours. Sometimes this means that you will be required to shift to another completely different setting or even change the context of the negotiation process with the objective of neutralizing the other person. For example, you can decide to do something like read a newspaper or go out for a movie.

6.   When the process turns personal, switch back to strictly business.

Negotiations can sometimes get personal or too emotional. When this happens during the process, you should always remind yourself that it is natural for the other person to try to get his way. This attitude should not startle you. What you should do instead is ensure that you keep things stringently business oriented.

Chapter # 5: Getting What You Want; Life concepts

In this chapter, we are going to discuss the relevant life concepts that will help you achieve your objectives, how to overcome life obstacles in order to achieve your goals, and about being responsible.

Prolific life concepts

The sooner you start to embrace productive life concepts, the faster you will start to achieve your goals and objectives. The most useful concept that you will have to observe, concerns the matter of developing your own life plan. The reason that makes me root for this approach is because a life plan is really easy to make since it will always remind you of what you should improve on, what you'd want to have, and what you want to be like in the future. The process of making one is really easy; just follows these simple steps:

1.   Rate your life

State whether or not you are honestly satisfied with your life. You do not have to share this information with others.

2.   Summarize your current state of affairs

Consider your career, health, spirituality, finances, relationships, and your emotional state. If there's a need, you can add any other areas that you find to be significant in your life.

3.   State what makes you happy and in high spirits

Take account of the people, situations, activities, and choices that bring joy in your life and also the things that make you laugh or smile. State what you enjoy doing and all the things that are flourishing in your life.

4.   Describe the things that make you sad

State what behaviors, people, situations, or choices that induce strain or stress into your life. There's not a single human being that does not have life toxins that drain away his life force.

5.   Narrate all the things that are not working in your life

Identify and state the obstacles that are preventing you from attaining your goals. You need to consider the constant challenges and conflicts in your life, for example, too much weight or lack of fitness.

6.   Describe what your preferred life would resemble

Portray, in subtle elements, the sort of life that would really make you ecstatic in the future. Describe what activities you would like to be doing, the person with whom you would like to share your fruitful life with, and how you expect to feel once you've achieved your objectives. It is essential for you to be transparent about what you truly want in your future.

7.   Outline what you need in order to achieve your goals

Consider what needs to occur for you to get from your current state to where you need to be. It does not have to be an itemized activity plan; however, you have to characterize your objectives. Reflect on the tendencies that you'd like to embrace or ways that may change your mindset or situation.

Lastly, we are going to discuss how to overcome obstacles that prevent us from achieving our goals and objectives

Tips on Beating Obstacles

I.   Examine behavior patters

Humans are creatures of propensity, effortlessly slipping back into practices that they acquire over time through learning and practice. Disappointingly, a hefty portion of these practices are not useful, and for the most part, they deter us from accomplishing our objectives. In actuality, these behavior patterns may be the most compelling reasons that make you not able to achieve your life goals.

II.   Be mindful of boundaries

You have to analyze your past disappointments in order to realize what has stopped you from achieving your goals or what prevented you from experiencing positive change in the past. Ultimately, in the event that you need a different result, you will have to dispose of the hindrances that block your achievements.

III.   Prepare in advance

Develop a strategy that will permit you to overcome snags before they even happen in the first place. Craft techniques and convey them before issues begin to emerge. This is a great way to deal with or take care of obstacles, as compared to the resolution of using willpower all the time.

IV.   Watch out for triggers

Watch out for situations that will make you backslide to pointless habits. Understand that on the off chance that you backslide, the chances of accomplishing your objectives will diminish, particularly if any of those goals include you staying drug-free.

Chapter # 6: The Law of Attraction

In this chapter, we will discuss how to effectively use the law of attraction to attain your goals. For those readers who don't know the meaning of the law of attraction, it basically implies that when you constantly have constructive thoughts and desires, you normally draw in constructive things, individuals, and occasions into your life. However, if you decide to linger onto negative contemplative ideas and desires, you'll draw in negative experiences into your life.

Suppose you have an objective that you need to accomplish, regardless of what it might be, and you need to make inquiries concerning ways that will help you to achieve your goal. You have to make inquiries to the appropriate individuals, and lastly, this law requires you to request the universe to reward you with your aspirations. Keep in mind that the key is not only to ask, but also to trust that when you do, you will eventually get what you are looking for.

If you have doubts in your heart while making the request, your goal won't succeed as expected. However, if you don't doubt the certainty that you will achieve your ambitions, and you go about as though you already have what you want, with time you will witness your goals come to light.

Essential Steps to follow

The Law of Attraction is an exceptionally basic ideology, however not everybody succeeds at mastering its use. If you've never really tried to apply and observe this law at work, you need to give it a try by following these steps:

❖　　　Envision yourself achieving your objectives on a regular basis.

❖　　　Imagine how your life will change once you get what you want.

- ❖   Maintain your focus throughout the journey.

- ❖   Create a list of small decisions that you intend to make, in order to lead to your end goal.

- ❖   Express your gratitude to the universe on a daily basis, like you've already gotten what you want.

III. Research Findings

Chapter # 7: Routine of a Successful Individual

In order to transform yourself into a prosperous guy who always achieves his goals, you will have to embrace the lifestyle associated with success. The best way to do this is to know how a successful person operates on a daily basis.

The ultimate goal of this chapter is help you to create a routine or schedule that will constantly reward you for any successful thing that happens in your life; be it big or small. Through this routine, you can develop your own schedule that will propel you towards achieving your own objectives.

Rise up on time

Individuals, who achieve their life goals, wake up on time. This is because they start their day on time and have the extra time they require to get things done. They face the day prepared for whatever comes their way.

Exercise Regularly

Exercise, unquestionably, is a part of the normal regimen of a successful individual's routine. It makes them be proactive, and keeps the body healthy.

On the off chance that you can't practice in the morning, get it in around lunchtime, or in the early hours of the evening. Don't overexert yourself in light of the fact that it may set you back.

Living a healthy lifestyle

In order to live a balanced lifestyle, prosperous people avoid constantly putting work in their daily program. They set aside some time for their family and themselves. Think of it as a method for energizing your body and life in general.

If you are constantly working, you are passing up a great opportunity. Personal time and space is vital, especially so that you can have time reflect on and survey your life. This is the perfect the time to develop new procedures for your success venture.

About Procrastination Habits

If there's a hustle that you keep postponing, then it's time for you to change this particular habit, so that you can become a fruitful individual. You will have to begin and complete any work you've been postponing to the best of your capacity.

Invest in yourself

Like many prosperous individuals, educate yourself, network with other productive people, invest in affiliations, reflect on spiritual matters, and deal with your physical and emotional wellness.

Sharing

As the precept goes, favored are the ones who impart their food offerings to those that are less fortunate in the society. Do your best to change the life of those that are poor and in need of assistance.

Chapter # 8: Successful Lifelong Objectives

In conclusion, it is useful to have fruitful objectives and goals. This is the only way that you will achieve them. In this chapter, we will discuss the general, but relevant, objectives that you need to observe in your life.

As indicated by Vedic's reasoning on humans, life has a clear and definite purpose. In this segment, we will talk about the four most applicable aspirations that nearly everyone has in life.

1.   Nobility or Righteousness

2.   Wealth Acquisition

3.   Satisfaction of Noble Desires

4.   Freedom or Liberation

It is fundamental to have the best possible conception concerning these aspirations. We shall describe the two initial objectives of interest since they are the most essential to drive anyone to get what he wants:

Nobility or Righteousness

This is the foremost quest of life. If you feel different about my opinion, please find time to reevaluate your goals and reconsider. Trust me, you'll have to make it your principal goal. This important virtue has two elements:

a)   Genuine confidence and commitment to God, as every single respectable quality originates from God.

b)   Practice of honesty in life.

The essential standards of Righteousness incorporate:

1. **Patience**:

It is the quality to resist the urge to panic and remain composed in all circumstances.

2. **Mind control**:

People ought to practice full control over their psyche, especially people that possess anxious and evolving minds.

3. **Absolution**:

This is a virtue that you need to develop in order to be an individual who is morally and physically strong. In any case, it is not alluring to pardon a person who habitually does wrong things.

4. **Cleanliness**:

You ought to keep the body, mind, and physical environment clean and unadulterated.

5.   Intelligence:

You should dependably attempt to pick up cleverness through study, self experience, and savvy organization.

6.   Control of Senses:

You must keep your sense of activity and knowledge under control and turn yourself into your own master.

7.   Information and knowledge:

You ought to be educated on both physical and other worldly domains from every conceivable source.

8.   Truth:

One should practice truth in thought, words, and deed

Wealth Acquisition

The acquirement of wealth is the second most critical interest or goal of human life. The following explains the original forms of wealth:

1.   Knowledge: Material Knowledge identifies with our common life, necessities, and exercises, while spiritual or profound information identifies with our soul, God, and internal life. Material knowledge is important to live a common life and it can be increased through competent education, extensive scholarly pursuit, and regular acquaintance. Be that as it may, the spiritual knowledge is so hard to obtain and it usually prompts self acknowledgment. If you want to acquire this type of knowledge, then you should opt to practice some yoga.

2. **Health**: You need to secure and practice the knowledge of achieving great health, which incorporates the prosperity of physical, mental, and emotional levels. Proper nourishment, general exercise, and sound reasoning are a portion of the basics of good well being.

3. **Contentment**: This gives you mental neutrality and proper moral strength, so that you are able to resist the urge to panic under any circumstance.

4. **Material Wealth**; Material wealth ought to be gained through righteousness. Money also should be utilized for beneficent or charitable purposes. It should not be exhausted for unnecessary necessities or extravagances. Lastly, you shouldn't become a victim of the material riches, but rather be its master.

Conclusion

I trust that this book had the capacity help you comprehend all that you need to know about achieving your life goals and objectives. In particular, it illuminated you on how useful it can be to pick up a proactive, stress-free life that will help you be more successful.

The next step is for you to put into practice what you have learnt in this book, and experience the striking impact it can have in your life and general body well being. Hence, it is your obligation to give it a shot and acknowledge how influential it can prove to be.

Author Bio

Muhammad Usman is a distinguished medical graduate of Allama Iqbal medical college (AIMC). He is a professional writer who has been in the field for more than 4 years. During this time he has produced 10,000+ articles, blogs, and eBooks on various niches related to diseases, health, fitness, nutrition, and well-being. He is a regular contributor to several journals related to medicine and surgery. He is the editor of several journals and newspapers.

Check out some of the other JD-Biz Publishing books
Gardening Series on Amazon

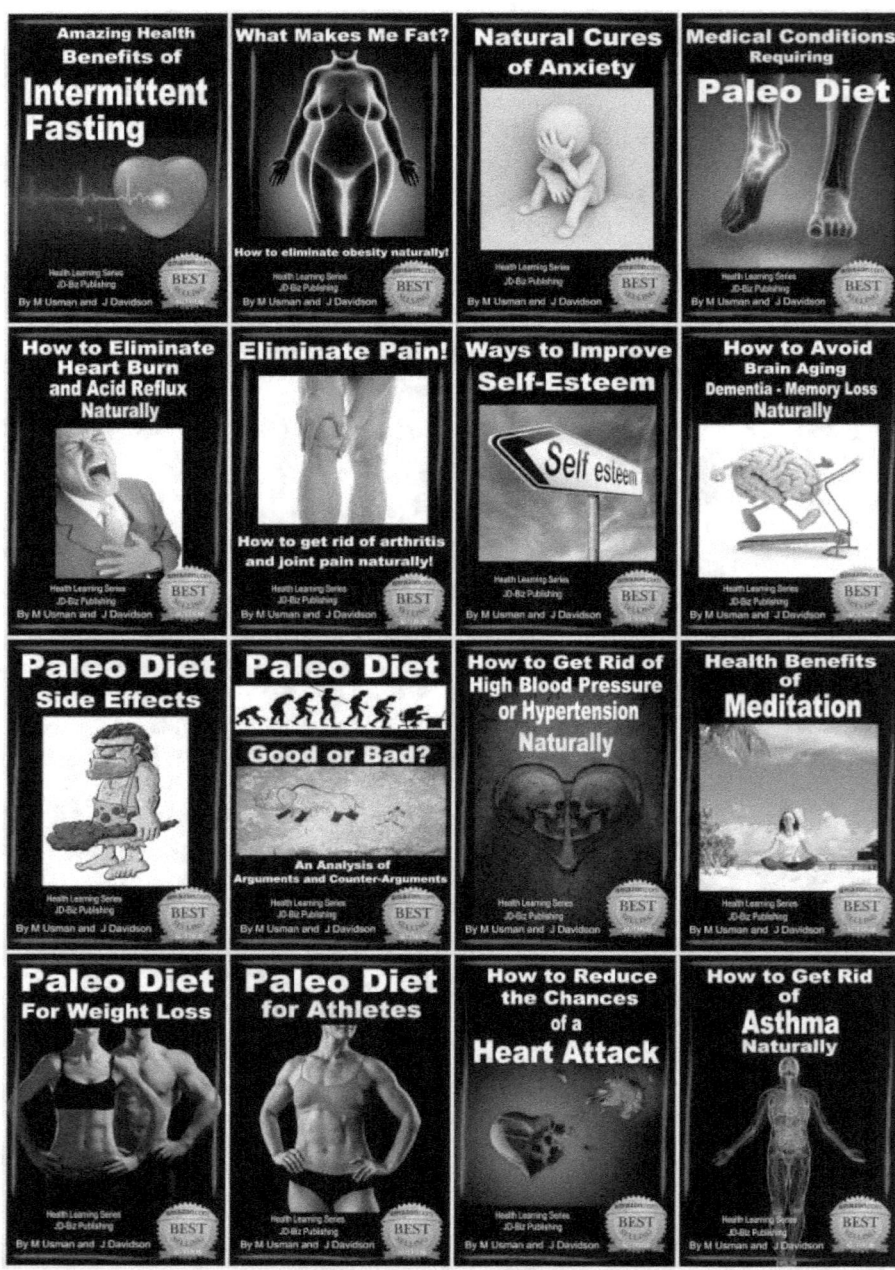

Learn To Draw Series

How to Build and Plan Books

Our books are available at

1. Amazon.com

2. Barnes and Noble

3. Itunes

4. Kobo

5. Smashwords

6. Google Play Books

Download Free Books!
http://MendonCottageBooks.com

Publisher

JD-Biz Corp

P O Box 374

Mendon, Utah 84325

http://www.jd-biz.com/

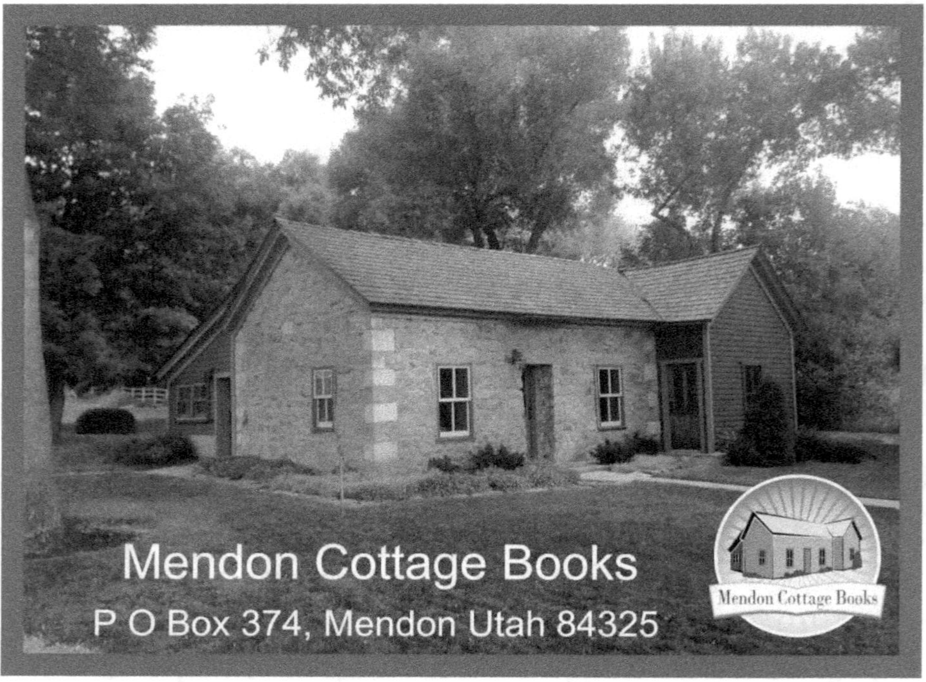

Mendon Cottage Books

P O Box 374, Mendon Utah 84325

www.ingramcontent.com/pod-product-compliance
Lightning Source LLC
Chambersburg PA
CBHW071141280526
45787CB00003B/1364